WOMEN BEHAVING
COURAGEOUSLY

The Workbook

Ann Andrews

Published by Activity Press

Contact author: www.annandrews.co.nz

ISBN 9780958263498 (paperback)

This workbook is dedicated to women who are tired of being tired.

Women the world over are making the courageous decision to cast off their traditional role of trying to be everything to everybody and standing up for a future that encourages them to become the fully actualised women they were born to be.

C O N T E N T S

Introduction

I'd worked for over 30+ years in the corporate world as an HR manager and subsequently as an HR consultant. I'd written numerous books over those years showing managers and owners how to build high performing teams: how to deal with conflict in teams and more particularly, how to be leaders rather than managers.

One day, a female neighbour asked if I'd written any books for women in leadership. She was working with one of the big banks and men were always given promotional priority over the female staff. I hadn't written any books for women, but then Covid hit and here in NZ we went into our very first lock-down, so I used the opportunity to write *Women Behaving Courageously: How gutsy women, young and old are transforming the world.*

At the book launch numerous women stayed behind to ask me if I ran workshops for women. At that stage I didn't and so I decided that I would.

I prepared for the first half day session I'd promoted by hunting out all my 'leadership' material given that the book had been written for a woman in the banking sector who wanted to better understand 'leadership' skills. On the day of the very first session and before I ran what I assumed the attendees wanted (leadership skills), I decided to ask each woman to introduce themselves and to let the group know what they wanted from my session.

Women are enormously honest. Every single woman there told me they wanted help with:

► Self-worth

► Guilt

► Exhaustion

The attendees were all professional women, most were working in the corporate world; some attendees were successfully running their own businesses, so to say I was stunned is an understatement. I promptly ditched all the material I'd planned and shared everything I knew about self-worth, guilt, and exhaustion.

Since that first eye-opening session, I've conducted several workshops and then because of another Covid lock-down and a waiting list of women who wanted to attend my sessions I took the sessions online.

This workbook then, is a result of those heart-breaking and heart-warming sessions where smart women shared their stories of always putting themselves last: always putting other people's dreams before theirs: deciding somewhere along the journey of their lives, that they weren't 'worth' success or wealth and were literally trained from birth never to put themselves first.

You're about to take your first test.

On the next page you will find the pre-course questionnaire I sent to every woman who was planning to attend either my live workshops or my online webinars. Answering these questions before you start on the workbook is important – you will gain a sense of not only where you're losing your energy but also, the areas you want to start working on, so you don't keep minimising your worth.

Please be honest with yourself.

It's also important that you sign and date the questionnaire. Doing this will hold you accountable for the changes you say you want to make, particularly if you take on a support person to keep you on track. They too will want to know you are 100% committed to changing self-defeating behaviours.

This workbook is designed to fall into three categories:

▶ Your past

▶ Your present

▶ Your future

Pre-course questionnaire

1. What aspects of your life are not working for you right now?

....

2. What would you like MORE of in your life?

....

3. What would you like LESS of in your life?

....

4. Do you have issues with any of the following (rank 0–10):

    0–3 Occasionally
    4–6 Sometimes
    7–8 Often
    9–10 All the time

    ▶ Asking for help ....

    ▶ Feelings of inadequacy ....

    ▶ Feeling on the outside looking in ....

    ▶ Feeling empty or invisible ....

    ▶ Feeling uncomfortable in social situations ....

    ▶ Difficulty setting/sticking to goals ....

    ▶ Difficulty making decisions ....

    ▶ Judging yourself more harshly than you judge others ....

    ▶ Beating yourself up if you make a mistake ....

    ▶ Never feeling 'enough' ....

    ▶ Not knowing what I want or would be good at ....

5. What is ONE thing you want to work on as you go through this workbook?

....

6. Who will you ask to support you as you make the necessary changes?

   ....

7. What are your greatest fears/concerns/self-doubts around achieving your goal? ....

8. Are you willing to give 100% to this workbook? Yes   Mostly   No

Signed .... Date ....

SESSION ONE:
Understanding your past

'Don't spend your life believing a story about yourself that you didn't write, that's been fed to you – that simply you've accepted, embedded and added to. Let the story go and there beneath is the real you ... and your unique gifts, heart and path that await you.'

— Rasheed Ogunlaru

Exploring feelings of self-worth, guilt and exhaustion

Self-worth is defined by **Merriam-Webster** as: *"a feeling that you're a good person who deserves to be treated with respect".*

When I asked participants to explain why they felt they needed help with feelings of low 'self-worth' their responses were along the lines of:

▶ I'm always expected to put my needs behind the needs of everyone in my family. I feel like a doormat

▶ My boss treats the males in our office way more respectfully than he treats the females – he makes me feel 'worthless'

▶ Every time I try to sign up for workshops on personal growth, my husband mocks me

▶ I'm knee deep in doing a Uni paper on top of a full-time job yet my mother expects me to fit in her grocery shopping and trips to the Dr while my brother doesn't lift a finger to help her

Guilt is when we feel we've let someone down, or not done something we promised to do or didn't do that 'something' the way we know we 'should' have done it. It's the awful feeling in the pit of our stomach; a feeling that can keep us awake at night and even start to cause us health issues.

The 'guilt' feelings women on my workshops shared were:

▶ Feeling guilty about neglecting my children when my boss asks me to work overtime even though we desperately need the extra income

▶ Feeling guilty when I'm taking time out with my children because I 'should' be concentrating on that exam paper that's due shortly

▶ Feeling guilty that my husband/partner was made redundant and I'm asking him/her to do the household chores I'd normally do because he/she is now home all day and I'm not

Exhaustion. Even when I mentioned this word, women's shoulders would slump, and their heads would fall forward. I asked why they were exhausted and almost had to stand back when they unleashed their outrage:

▶ Cos it seems I'm the only person in my household who can shop, do the washing, make the kids lunches, drop them off at school, attend parent evenings, go to sports event, take them to the Drs and the dentist

▶ Because my husband/partner works long hours and thinks my job is just 9 – 5 and why am I always so tired and why isn't his/her dinner on the table when he/she gets home?

▶ Because my mother has a severe case of learned helplessness, she has a car, never drives it so I must pick her up to take her shopping and ferry her to all her many Drs appointments

▶ Because my sister is constantly borrowing money from me and rarely pays it back. I'm struggling financially too

When I'm running a live workshop, I now leave quite a chunk of time to let women vent their rage and fury over how much they are expected to do and how utterly worn out they are. It's healthy to get this pain and hurt out of our systems.

Investigating your family of origin

When you were a little girl, what messages were you given by your parents and extended family? Fill in the blanks:

- ▶ Girls can't ....
- ▶ Girls shouldn't ....
- ▶ Girls must never ....
- ▶ Women mustn't ....
- ▶ Women shouldn't ....
- ▶ It's a woman's job to ....

How did/does this make you feel?

....

How has this affected your life?

....

Our family of origin lays the foundations for our early programming so that forever as we go forward in our lives, we'll have that little voice in our head that keeps reminding us 'mum said girls shouldn't' or gran was very clear 'Women mustn't'.

Think about:

- ▶ What is your place in the family? (Youngest, oldest, middle, only child, twin)? Our place in the family has huge bearing on how we are treated and how we live out our lives. Oldest children are expected to take on responsibilities for younger children. Youngest child is often given way more freedom than previous siblings. Middle children can feel invisible. Twins tend to live in their own world and isolate themselves from their siblings, and only children are often lonely and can become insular.

  ....

- ▶ What country were you born in? ....
- ▶ What culture or religion were you born into? ....
- ▶ What year were you born? ....
- ▶ What were the societal norms for girls at that time? ....

▶ What expectations were set for the females in your family (or not)?
....

▶ Which schools did you attend (all girls, a religious school, boy and girls mixed)? ....

▶ What teachers did you have? (Ones that encouraged you or treated you as invisible or even labeled you a troublemaker.) ....

▶ What sort of friends did you have? (Good, bad and/or dangerous)..................

▶ What do you know about your parents' lives?
....

▶ What do you know about your grandparents' and even great-grandparents' lives? ....

All these aspects of your childhood plus the background and beliefs of generations of your family have moulded you. The question is ARE YOU HAPPY WITH WHO YOU ARE RIGHT NOW? If you are, great, if you're not, then let's get to work.

A happiness/contentment test

On a scale of 0–10, how happy and content are you with your life?

0–3 = utterly miserable. 4–6 = OK but know my life could be way better. 7–10 = my life is pretty good, but I would like to stretch my wings to see what else I'm capable of doing. Explain:

0–3 (Why?) ....
....

4– 6 (Why?)...
....

7–10 (Your what next?)...
....

Unravelling your early programming

All the messages that go into our subconscious from birth till the age of 7 become our 'early programming'. It was Aristotle who said, 'Give me a child till they are 7 and I'll show you the adult'.

The problem is that in these early years we have no way of rationalising what we're being taught or what we're being told. If mum doesn't want us because she already has too many children, or can't afford more children, then the first seed planted into our being is that we are not wanted and we're not yet even the size of a pin head.

Once we're born, if dad says we are stupid and useless regularly enough, then that will become our self-belief. If our mother says that 'girls should be nice and look after everyone else' then that's what we are programmed to do and will feel guilty if we go against our mother.

After age 7 we start to go out into a larger world. We are now at school and may be invited to a friend's home where we may see a different culture, different rules, different ways of being treated. When we then become adults, we may feel torn and confused. Our programming told us that 'girls couldn't' yet I'm now seeing my female friends doing all manner of amazing things I was told I couldn't, mustn't and shouldn't do. This dichotomy causes internal conflict and guilt. If I adhere to my own programming then I'll live to the limits I've been set; if I decide NOT to do that, I may feel I'm being disloyal to my family. Which leads to us living out:

Learned behaviours and limiting beliefs

We may live out our programming for many years. We may marry as we were expected to do, we may try to look after our family and put their needs before ours, we may decide not to pursue a career or start a business because we were told girls 'Shouldn't do that'.

Eventually living someone else's expectations of us will take a toll and because we can never live up to someone else's version of us, our internal message will become 'I don't measure up'.

> *'You don't know who you are; you just know what they've told you about who you are!'*
>
> — Maddy Malhotra

A case study

I worked as a counsellor many years ago, and one young woman stands out in my memory as a way to explain why it's vital that we understand our early years and deal with the baggage we're carrying around with us as a result of those early years.

Sarah had picked up an ad I ran in the local newspaper for one of my early women's workshops. She asked if she could come and see me one on one to talk over her issues before she decided on attending a public workshop. I had several sessions with Sarah as we explored her concerns: low self-worth, inability to keep a job or sustain healthy relationships, poor sleep patterns, general feelings of low energy and a drastically poor relationship with her family. She felt she was the black sheep of the entire family and was always letting everyone down.

I asked her to tell me about her childhood and immediately the tears flowed.

Sarah's story:

Sarah is a middle child with an older sister and a younger brother. Her sister was born two years before her and her brother five years after her. She felt she didn't belong in the family; that she was an outsider; that her sister and brother were both successful while she couldn't hold down a job for more than a few months at a time so of course her family thought she was a loser.

I asked about her earliest memories, and now the tears really flowed. She talked about the fact that there are literally no family photos of her as a baby. Her parents lounge still has photos of her sister as a baby and masses of her brother as a baby, but not even one of her until she reached school age. I asked why she thought that was. She felt it was because she had been an ugly baby and she wasn't worth photographing.

I urged Sarah to ask her parents why there were no photos of her rather than make such a sad assumption.

She discovered that when her sister was born, her parents had a cheap camera and this being their first child, the camera was always at the ready. Just before Sarah was born her father had lost his job, enforcing a move to cheaper housing. Sarah was born at a particularly difficult time in their lives, the camera was broken in the house move and they couldn't afford to replace it. Time passed, dad found another job, their first son was born, and a new camera was purchased.

So, a loss of job and an enforced move had caused some tough times and a broken camera. Sarah had lived her entire life carrying her 'not worth' story when in fact she was loved just as much as her siblings.

I describe our early memories as looking through a keyhole. We see just a tiny part of the room beyond the door. Once we ask our questions and open the door, all manner of explanations surface.

Once Sarah understood what had happened, she was able to let go of her 'not worth' feelings and to start re-building her entire being based on the real facts around her early years.

'When you hold onto a script that doesn't serve you,
you leave no space to write a new one that does.'

—Jennifer Ho

SESSION TWO:
Making sense of your present

'If you never heal from what hurt you, you'll bleed
on people who didn't cut you.'

— Unknown

Patterns you've developed for better or worse

I've worked with numerous people who've said, 'Look I'm fine, I don't need counselling, you can't change the past just best to get on with things.' The problem is that if we don't deal with our past, it will deal TO us, just as it was dealing to Sarah.

If we don't get clear on those early years, then our early programming, traumas and beliefs eventually lead to us developing 'patterns' of behaviour that can become incredibly destructive.

Check the list below:

1. Finances: (Example, I live in a poverty/scarcity trap, or I always spend more than I earn no matter how much I earn)

2. Romantic relationships: (Example, I attract and am attracted to the same type of partner repeatedly even though I know such partners are bad for me)

3. Family dramas: (Example, siblings constantly borrow off me and never pay me back. My parents rely on me for everything even though I have 3 siblings)

4. Significant 'other' relationships: (My friendships don't seem to last very long,

and I don't know why)

5. Over-indulgence: (Alcohol, food, shopping, sex)

6. Career challenges: (I keep getting stuck with abusive bosses or dead-end jobs)

7. Decision-making: (I spend my life procrastinating and miss so many opportunities)

8. Health issues: (I catch every cold that's going)

RANK IN ORDER OF YOUR DESIRE TO CHANGE YOUR PATTERNS (don't try to work on too many areas at once)

1. ....

2. ....

3. ....

4. ....

5. ....

6. ....

7. ....

8. ....

*'If you always do what you've always done, you'll
always get what you've always got.'*

— Jessie Potter

SESSION THREE:
Reclaiming your energy

'It wasn't that she was sad—sadness had very little to do with it, really, considering that most of the time, she felt close to nothing at all. Feeling required nerves, connections, sensory input. The only thing she felt was numb. And tired. Yes, she very frequently felt tired.'

— Nenia Campbell

Learning to say NO

Whenever I've spoken to a woman's group or conducted one of my workshops, I always suggest that perhaps it's time we women learned how to say no. A ripple WILL go through the audience. I've even had women call out to say or 'I can't say no to my husband/boss/children/mother/father/sister/ .... (Fill in the blank). To which I reply, 'Why can't you?' which gets the fluttering around the room to rise to very interesting proportions. The response is invariably 'Well that's not very nice'.

And there we have the woman's dilemma. We've been programmed to be 'nice' no matter the cost to our health, well-being, personal aspirations, or sanity. By never saying no and always picking up the pieces of everyone's lives, we are actually encouraging people to become dependent on us. We become 'needed'. Which in some perverse way is supposed to make women feel important when it's increasingly clear that what being needed is doing is causing women to feel

EXHAUSTED.

I then ask the question 'How many of the people in your life are perfectly capable of doing all those things they ask you to do for them?'. And the room invariably becomes very quiet. Apart from babies, toddlers, and children under 6/7, most humans can be taught to do most of the things we are doing for them. I'm not saying don't 'help', I'm saying don't become a dumping ground for things others are perfectly capable of doing for themselves.

Why we fear saying NO

▶ We fear upsetting people

▶ We don't know HOW to say no

▶ We fear the reactions to us saying no

▶ We fear the consequences of saying no

Reactions to you saying NO

▶ Anger/shock/outrage (how dare you)

▶ You used to be so nice

▶ You've become so selfish

▶ Being given the silent treatment (for hours, days, weeks, months or for ever)

Why it's vital that we learn to say NO

We need to learn to say NO, so we have the time and energy to be able to say YES to the person we want to become: to grasp the opportunities that come our way which we keep turning down because we have no time or energy: to get out of the vicious cycle of being bottom of the pile.

Step 1: Learning to say No. WARNING: These steps are designed to deal with adults not children

Choose an easy person and an easy situation first. No-one suggests that you start saying no loudly, firmly, aggressively, or even immediately. That really would be a shock and probably wouldn't get you the best outcome. Step 1 in learning to say no is to offer a compromise:

▶ Stay calm and use a soft tone

- ▶ I can't do X but I could do Y – would that work for you?
- ▶ I can't do that right now, but I could do it ....

Step 2: Plan ahead

Take some time upfront to get clear on the things you really want to stop doing for other people. Learn to say no assertively not aggressively. The 'who' is important here – boss, co-worker, friend, relative, partner – clearly you can't necessarily use the same strategy for a boss that you would use say, for your sister.

Step 3: Pick your battles.

Start to quietly but firmly plant the seeds that from this day forward you are not going to hand your life over to someone else to do things they are perfectly capable of doing themselves.

Step 4: Begin to set your boundaries

A wonderful technique is to become a 'broken record'

- ▶ 'Remember I said I was happy to do X but I couldn't do Y'
- ▶ 'I'll do it this time, but I'd rather you ask .... next time'
- ▶ 'Have a think about what I've said (if it looks as though things are turning ugly) how about we have some time out, have a think about the alternatives I've suggested and let's see if we can find some workable compromises'

Time out tips:

- ▶ 'I'll leave that with you but please have a think about what I've suggested.'
- ▶ 'If there's a better way let me know.'
- ▶ 'It's OK for us to agree to disagree.'

Step 5: Use the power of the pause

When you've made your 'Remember I said ...' statement, please learn to shut up. Our 'niceness' tends to want to fill silence with all manner of excuses and rationale – don't fall into that trap. Stay quiet and the person will hopefully get the message. If not, use broken record again 'Remember I said I could ....' at which point they may huff and puff and possibly even walk away. Well done, you stood your ground, didn't back down and you'll now live to fight another day.

Step 6: The DON'TS

1. Don't get into arguments

2. Don't ever put yourself into a dangerous situation

3. Don't give up, if you don't get the message over the first time, it's OK to try again later

I had one gorgeous example on one of my online courses where I asked, 'What do people ask you to do that drives you insane?' and a gorgeous older lady said, 'My husband never writes anything down and forgets appointments, he will ask me "When am I supposed to be going to the dentist?" It drives me mad.'

However, she was encouraging the behaviour because she would write things in HER diary, so his dates didn't clash with other things in their lives.

My suggestion was as a first step, to write the dates in HIS diary so the next time he asked she could say 'it's in your diary', and then walk away.

One small step for womankind, one giant leap for her sanity.

Step 7: Don't always be the one that volunteers

Another situation arose on one of my webinars, one of the lovely women on the session was the eldest in a big family, all her siblings were married, she was not, their mother was aging and regularly needed someone to take her to Dr's appointments.

This lovely woman always stepped up because she felt that because she was the oldest it was her responsibility and being single meant she had no other calls on her time, which simply wasn't so. This lady is a sole trader whilst all her siblings have well-paid jobs, so when she became the person who took over all her mother's appointments, she was missing out on potential business and putting herself in financial jeopardy.

We asked her NOT to volunteer for her mother's next appointment and she didn't. A young sister-in-law was delighted to offer, she was bored at home and wanted to get to know her mother-in-law better.

> *'I got used to everyone needing me, to them relying on me and now that I wasn't needed anymore, I simply didn't know what to do with myself.'*
>
> — Jay Crownover

Your Action Plan

Who do I need to speak to first?

....

What are they asking me to do that I don't want to do any longer?

....

How will I say it? 'I can't do that for you on a regular basis any longer (or whatever it is you plan to say)?'

....

What reaction am I likely to get when I say NO?

....

How will I deal with that reaction?

....

What workable compromises can I suggest?

....

Who could I role play with?

....

Step 7: Review. Well done for giving it a go

Did it go well, OK or really badly?

....

What did you do that you are proud of?

....

What will you do differently if you get another chance?

....

Did you get your message across even partially?

....

Step 8: What if the discussion went badly?

Our fear is that the person may never speak to us again. In some cases that could be good news, but if it isn't good news and you are now knee deep in the person not speaking to you, here are some tips:

1. Give the person some time and space

2. If they get in touch with you to talk things over – great news – rinse and repeat everything you said first time around with whatever modifications you see fit (without backing down).

3. If you don't hear from them after a reasonable period, contact them. A call, a text, even a wee card saying 'How are you? Hope you're OK? How about we have a coffee?'

4. If they ignore your attempt to bridge the gap, leave it a while longer. If the relationship is important to you, it's OK to try again – without backing down.

This stuff isn't easy. In my experience if I let someone know I'm not happy about something, the first time they may not hear me, the second time they may not hear me but if after 3 attempts to bridge the gap without backing down they still haven't heard me, then sadly, they probably never will.

It's at this point we must think through our own 'what next'.

Is the relationship sufficiently important to you that you can live with the person's quirks (without you being used or abused)? If you can, then you may have to make some allowances, if you can't then you may have to walk away or if it's a family member, only see them on special occasions.

YOU must be more important to yourself than any other human being.

Step 9: Prepare, plan, prepare some more

▶ Practice

▶ Role play with someone you trust

▶ Test some neutral phrases

▶ Who will you decide to speak to first?

▶ What likely reactions do you expect (anger, tears, silent treatment)?

▶ What strategy will you use to deal with that (pause, broken record, time out)?

▶ Practice, practice, practice

▶ If at first, you don't succeed – don't quit (plant the seed for next time)

- ▶ Use 'time out' if things get too heated, but REVISIT the conversation
- ▶ Live to fight another day
- ▶ Be 100% determined
- ▶ Purchase a journal (more on this down-track)

'I myself have never been able to find out precisely what feminism is: I only know that people call me a feminist whenever I express sentiments that differentiate me from a doormat.'

— Rebecca West

To summarise

What is the most valuable thing you've learned from this workbook so far?

What will you do with that knowledge?

....

What will your first change of behaviour be, starting tomorrow?

Who do you plan to ask to be your support person as you take that step?

Who do you need to learn tolerance towards?

What would be the win/win if you could work this out?

Who do you need to spend less time with?

Who do you need to let go of altogether?

How will you keep your levels of motivation and determination high if things don't go perfectly the first time you try these techniques?

Will you now decide, once and for all, that you are worth being treated with respect?

....

'The mind, once stretched by a new idea, never returns to its original dimensions.'

— Ralph Waldo Emerson

SESSION FOUR:
Designing your magnicent future

'Everyone has a calling, and your real job is to figure out as soon as possible what that is, who you were meant to be and to begin to honour that in the best way possible for yourself.

— Oprah

Daring to say YES

I once ran a workshop entitled 'I know I'm here to do something amazing, I just wish I could work out what that is!' and so many women showed up. There's a famous Richard Bach quote where he says, *'There's a test to find out if your life on earth is done, if you're alive it isn't!'*

I think we all want to make a difference, to look back on our lives and say, 'that was a ball' and/or 'I really did make a difference'.

Test: I asked what you wanted to be when you were a little girl?

Q: I wanted to be ....

Q: When/why did you give up? ....

Q: Who stole your dream? ....

Q: Can you re-vitalise that dream? ....

Q: Are you now settling for peace and quiet? ....

The most heartbreaking phrase in the English language – 'Ah yes BUT'

- ▶ I'm too old/too young

- ▶ I don't have the right qualifications

- ▶ My partner/mum/dad/sister/son/daughter/best friend wouldn't like it

- ▶ It's not the right time

- ▶ We can't afford it

- ▶ I'll do it when (the kids leave home/we pay off the mortgage/I finish paying for my car)

Simple ways to follow your dream

I'd been working with a team of ICU nurses. Our nursing population is getting older, and the pressures and stresses of ICU take a greater toll as we age.

One older nurse said that she 'dreamed' of running her own business growing and selling herbs. I asked why she wasn't doing that. And the old 'It's not the right time and we're still paying a mortgage' rationale came up. I asked if she could reduce her hours by just half a day a week so she could prepare her herbs for a local fair which ran every week near her.

After a bit of humming and pontificating, she realized she could do that, and so she did. She then moved to 4 days a week, then 3 until eventually she realized she could make almost as much money selling herbs as she made in her nursing job and was way happier and much healthier doing what she loved. It's amazing what we can do if we 'chunk' things down into bite-sized pieces.

One small step really can launch a giant leap given time and determination.

- ▶ Turn a passion into a hobby

- ▶ Turn a hobby into small business

- ▶ Turn your passion into your life's purpose

Signs that you are READY

- ▶ Your never-ending patterns (self-sabotage, fear of failure) are happening faster and hitting you more forcefully each time

▶ You have constant feelings of discontent, worthlessness, exhaustion

▶ You are feeling a sense of urgency

▶ You are starting to have health issues – headaches, lethargy, insomnia, digestive issues, blood pressure, migraines

Messages are all around you

▶ Books seem to leap off the shelves at you

▶ Chance meetings with the exact right person with the exact right message you need to hear

▶ Coincidences – you're thinking of going to Uni and you meet a friend who has just started studying the same paper you dearly want to do

▶ Unusual dreams

Writing the book *Women Behaving Courageously* came about because of that chance conversation with a neighbour and three strange dreams.

Dream 1: I was driving down a road on the wrong side of the road going in the wrong direction. The coincidence was that I was meeting that very day with three friends and shared the dream with them. They all gave me the 'look', the look that says 'Mmmmm I wonder what that might mean, Ann?'

Dream 2: I was driving down the road on the right side of the road but still going in the wrong direction

Dream 3: I was driving on the right side of the road in the wrong direction but this time I got out of the car, looked over to my left and saw the road I should be on, and my neighbour was standing there waving at me.

I started writing the book the very next day.

> *'There are only two ways to live your life. One is as though nothing is a miracle, the other is as though everything is a miracle.'*

> — Albert Einstein

Warriors at Work

Definitions: A hero is a real or mythical person of real bravery who carries out extraordinary deeds: a warrior is a person who is actively engaged in battle, conflict or warfare, a soldier or combatant.

After the conversation with my neighbour, I pondered who had been my own heroes as I was growing up, and I thought of a variety of amazing women.

My earliest 'hero' memory was learning the story of Gladys Aylward – a cleaning lady who had a dream to go to China. Imagine the reactions she received when she shared that story with people around her. Gladys had never been to China, didn't speak the language and had no way of getting to China. Her story is absolutely staggering and was eventually made into a movie – *The Inn of the 6ᵗʰ Happiness*.

Florence Nightingale was a warrior: she came from a middle-class background in the days when 'nursing' was seen as the lowest of low professions. She ignored all the detractors, even defying her father to nurse in the Crimean War. She became famously known as 'the lady with the lamp' and changed the face of nursing, making it a reputable career path for young women to follow.

The Suffragettes were the epitome of 'heroes': they literally risked their lives in so many dangerous ways to ensure that women were finally given the right to vote. At that period in history, women were very much second-class citizens. If women inherited money or property from their parents and were married, their husbands now owned that wealth: they were to all intents and purposes, owned by their husbands.

These memories led me to thinking about our modern-day female warriors and heroes.

If you already have a copy of the original book, you will have met my 25 warriors, some will be familiar to you, others may not be so familiar. If you do NOT have a copy of the book, you can purchase one at:

www.annandrews.co.nz/product/women-behaving-courageously-2/.

I categorized my warrior women as follows:

Quiet Warriors: I chose Dame Jane Goodall and the late Ruth Bader Ginsburg

Gracious Warriors: I chose Christine Blasey Ford, Michelle Obama and Jacinda Ardern

Business Warriors: I chose Dame Anita Roddick and Melinda Gates

Unintentional Warriors: I chose Linda Ronstadt and Elissa Slotkin

Intellectual Warriors: I chose Elizabeth Warren, Malala Yousafzai and Angela Merkel

Laugh-in-your-face Warriors: I chose J.K. Rowling and Bette Midler

Rambunctious, LOUD and Unapologetic Warriors: I chose Emma Gonzalez and Alexandria Ocasio-Cortez

Never-Give-Up Warriors: I chose Jane Fonda and Lucy Lawless

Spiritual Warriors: I chose Louise Hay and Oprah Winfrey

The Bravest of Brave Warriors: I chose Marie Yovanovitch and Fiona Hill

Magnificent 'Don't-mess-with-me' Warriors: I chose Kamala Harris and Nancy Pelosi

The Warrior to beat ALL Warriors: I chose Greta Thunberg

'Fate whispers to the warrior, you cannot withstand the storm and woman shouts back I AM THE STORM'

— Unknown

A Warrior Woman Test

For the point of this exercise, which Warrior 'type' do you relate to?

....

What are you currently doing with that type of energy?

....

What more would you LIKE to do with that energy?

....

How to be all you are capable of being

What were your early aspirations? (I keep asking women this question until they re-member.)

....

What do you do now to relax?

....

Where does time stand still (an activity which takes you into your zone)?

....

What do people ask you to help with?

....

What would you happily do for free?

....

'You've been assigned this mountain so you can show others it can be moved.'

— Mel Robbins

A simple goal setting process

My ultimate vision (where I would like to be in 2 – 5 years)

....

Why that is so important to me?

....

What are my superpowers? (And you do have superpowers. If you are unsure what they are, ask your dearest friend, she will tell you.)

....

....

What behaviours will take me towards my vision?

....

....

What behaviours will take me away from my vision?

....

Where would I need to be in one year?

....

Where would I need to be in 6 months?

....

Where would I need to be in 3 months?

....

MY 30 DAY 'TO DO' LIST

....

....

....

....

....

The Life Changing Power of Journaling

1. **Keeping a journal** is one of the most powerful things you can do for yourself, particularly in times of confusion or pain.

I use my journal when I'm feeling angry, scared, confused, unsure, or any other emotion I am dealing with which leaves me feeling 'out of control'.

I ask myself:

- WHAT am I feeling? (I literally write until I gain clarity.)

- WHY am I feeling that?

- HOW will I deal with that feeling?

- WHEN will I deal with it?

Sometimes a situation is so tense or difficult that dealing with it head-on may not be possible. This is where your journal can be your soulmate, your best friend, your counsellor, and your guide.

It may feel that simply writing in a journal is a wimpish way out or even a cop-out. It isn't. On some cellular level, you are dealing with your situation. Often by writing out my problem and then going to sleep, it's almost as if my subconscious gives me an answer.

I may dream of a solution or even wake the next morning with a surprise solution, as I did with my dreams about being on the wrong road.

Sometimes this is the only way you can deal with an issue and dealing with an issue this way is perfectly OK.

2. **Record what you're GRATEFUL for.** Sometimes we get so bogged down in our day-to-day clutter we forget we have enormous amounts of things and people in our lives we can be thankful for.

3. **Thank someone every day.** Meister Eckhart once said, 'If the only prayer you said was thank you, that would be enough.'

4. **Try a 'forgiveness' exercise.** One of the women on my workshops had experienced a terrible relationship with her mum who had died several years before. She used her journal to explore that relationship, the good, bad and the sad. She decided to write a letter to her mum in her journal asking for forgiveness for not understanding the pain and baggage she knew her mother had suffered in HER family of origin.

She shared the forgiveness story at our next session and acknowledged she now felt as if a huge burden had been lifted off her back.

Write to the person you want to ask for forgiveness from, you will be staggered at the weight that lifts off your shoulders. If the person is still alive, you don't need to send it unless you choose to!

5. FORGIVE YOURSELF: We spend years beating ourselves up, berating ourselves, denigrating ourselves and we must stop doing that.

All our lives we've done the best we could, and after working through these exercises I hope you realise that your past does NOT determine your future.

YOU decide how you want the next stage of your life to be.

'You've been criticizing yourself for years and it hasn't worked. Try approving of yourself and see what happens.'

— Louise Hay

Quotes for when the going gets tough

'I believe that many modern women, my mother included, carry within them a whole secret New England cemetery, wherein they have quietly buried- in neat little rows- the personal dreams they have given up for their families.'

— Elizabeth Gilbert

'If you trade your authenticity for safety, you may experience anxiety, depression, eating disorders, addictions, rage, blame, resentment and inexplicable grief.'

— Brene Brown

'Don't ever feel bad for making a decision about your life that upsets other people. You are not responsible for their happiness. You're responsible for YOUR happiness. Anyone who wants you to live in misery should not be in your life anyway.'

— Isaiah Hankel

'Be thankful for what you have: you'll end up having more. If you concentrate on what you don't have, you'll never, ever have enough.'

— Oprah

'I am only one, but still I am one. I cannot do everything, but still I can do something; and because I cannot do everything, I will not refuse to do something that I can do.'

— Helen Keller

'If not me then who, if not now, then when?'

— Malcolm X (ish)

'Do one thing every day that scares you.'

— Eleanor Roosevelt

'You'll never know how strong you are until being strong is your only choice.'

— Bob Marley

'Don't cry because it's over, smile because it happened.'

— Dr Seuss

'You alone are enough; you have nothing to prove to anyone.'

— Maya Angelou

'The moment you are ready to quit, is the moment right before a miracle could happen.'

'I believe that the influence of women will save the world before every other power.'

— Lucy Stone

'The woman who does not need validation from anyone, is the most feared individual on the planet.'

— Mohadesa Najumi

'She remembered who she was, and the game changed.'

— Lala Delia

'Courage doesn't always roar, sometimes courage is the quiet voice at the end of the day saying, I'll try again tomorrow.'

— Mary Anne Radmaster

Some final thoughts

I believe we are all on this earth for a purpose. It doesn't have to be a lofty 'change-the-world' purpose, it may just be a purpose that says I want to make a difference in my corner of the world.

Your passion may be rescuing pets, it may be fostering children, it may be volunteering at your local Hospice shop. If it makes your heart sing, just do it. Don't sell yourself short by putting everyone else's needs and wants ahead of yours.

You are totally 'worth' it.

As I was closing off this workbook, I discovered an amazing quote I've adapted to reflect everything I've said so far. It sums up everything I believe in. Trust the process; trust your instincts; trust that the answers you seek will appear and trust totally that you can and do make a difference.

Head: I'm worried

Heart: Just relax

Head: But I'm totally lost and stressed now

Heart: Just follow me

Head: But I've never done this before and I'm not known for sticking to things and what if it goes wrong and things are worse than before, and what if I make a fool of myself and people laugh at my stupidity for thinking I could do this?

Heart: Trust me, this time I think we're on track

Soul: If you two would just shut up, I'd show you the map

Go well. Be courageous. Be daring. But above all else, do NOT die with your music still in you.

Ann Andrews

Further reading

Games People Play, Eric Berne MD

I'm OK – You're OK, Thomas A Harris MD

You Can Heal Your Life, Louise Hay

No, It's NOT OK, Tania Roxborogh and Kim Stephenson

Feel The Fear and Do It Anyway, Susan Jeffers

The Disease to Please, Harriet B. Braiker, PhD

The Life You Were Born to Live, Dan Millman

Book of the Heart: Meditations for the Restless Soul, Meister Eckhart

Other books by the author

Shift Your But (1999)

Finding the Square Root of a Banana (2000)

Did I Really Employ You? (2004)

My Dear Franchisees (2006)

Excellent Employment: Hiring the best people to help your business grow (2007)

Mum's the Word by Vanessa Sunde, Kenina Court and Ann Andrews (2007)

Lessons in Leadership: 50 Way to Avoid Falling into the 'Trump' Trap (2017)

Leaders Behaving Badly: What happens when ordinary people show up, stand up and speak up (2018)

Women Behaving Courageously: How gutsy women, young and old are transforming the world (2020)

About the author

Ann Andrews had a rocky start in her own life. Ann is illegitimate born at a time when it was not cool to be illegitimate.

Despite that, the first six years of her life were idyllic. She was brought up by her grandparents thinking they were her parents which was not unusual in those days. Then her real mother, who she thought was her big sister, married and Ann was taken to live with her newly discovered mother and stepfather.

Twelve truly horrendous years followed. At 18 Ann left home and never went back other than for short holidays to see her beloved grandparents.

Her life chugged along. She married, had two gorgeous children and then after 17 years her marriage fell apart.

By now Ann was living in a different country from her family, she had no job, no prospects of finding a job and no money. Pulling herself up by her bootstraps, she became a secretarial 'temp' and because of a hard-working work ethic instilled in her by her grandparents, rapidly rose through the ranks from being a personnel administrator to personnel assistant to personnel manager to becoming an HR manager to ultimately to setting up her own HR Consultancy which she ran successfully for over 30 years.

However, during those years of trying to survive as a solo parent and trying to feed her family, Ann had a major cancer scare. Fortunately, her doctor came from the Louise Hay school of healing and asked her when she was going to 'get her life sorted out?'

Imagine the shock of that question on top of a terrifying cancer diagnosis.

He went one step further and gave her a flyer for a weekend workshop designed to help her do just that. Ann attended the strange workshop and spent quite a few subsequent years in counselling. The aim of all that counselling was to deal with the buried trauma of those awful years with the stepfather from Hell.

Ann knows first-hand the cost of unresolved baggage. It almost cost her, her life.

After 30 years running her own business and having no more health scares, Ann was planning retirement, when she had the conversation which led to her writing *Women Behaving Courageously: How gutsy women, young and old are transforming the world* and the creation of those workshops for women, and ultimately, this workbook.

Her workshops are designed to help other women dragging around pain and trauma from a childhood they are still trying to come to terms with.

The sessions are designed to help women who find themselves in relationships that don't nourish them or in jobs that are beneath them and/or in situations where they keep repeating patterns of self-sabotage.

Ann is determined to help women short-circuit the pain of their unresolved stuff, so they don't have to drag the burden around for years as she did, because if a woman is carrying hurt, she will never blossom into the amazing woman she is capable of being.

Ann urges women of all ages, to remember this, her favourite quote of all:

'There's a vitality, a life force, an energy that is translated through you into action. And because there is only one of you in all of time, this expression is unique. If you block it, it will never exist again. It will be lost'.

— Martha Graham